For every WoMan who has doubted and every
WoMan who has triumphed over
adversity.

For Lily – my flower, my daughter.
Speak with courage and chase
your dreams with courage.

Inside

MOTHER

When I kiss your lips child
The spirit of my Mother is on my lips
When I wipe your tears girl
The spirit of my Mother is on my wiping hand

When I look at you Lily
I see the energy of my Mother in your eyes
When you laugh and get shy
I feel the timid, fun nature of my Mother in you

There's an invisible cord
Coiled in gold and motherly love
Entwined with worry and faithful expectation
A cord which ties us all together as One

When I stroke your face as you rest
I feel my Mother's hand tapping me to sleep
Soothing me, as I lay beside my own child
Hoping the same for you

LEELA'S LULLABY

I will watch over you
While you sleep tonight
I will watch over you
While you sleep tight

While you are sleeping
I'll be there for you
While you are sleeping
I will care for you

When the sun has gone
And the moon shines bright
I will watch over you
I will be your Light

I will watch over you
While you sleep tonight
I will watch over you
While you sleep tight

BIRTHING

Oh, new Life birthed!
Awareness arises and
So Love is borne
In Womb and Heart
So in child of thine.

THERE GO I

There, through free will and wanting, go I.
Grace of my God, say I.
My inner Divine and all it's knowing.
Takes me to chances and places,
People and spaces.

There, through free will and wanting, go I.
Chances we take, heartbreak may await.
But, for chance and purpose, risk I.
For the beauty of growth and good things
And the mayhaps of light go I.

Life is short, some say.
Those are the ones who live too fast.
Slow down my friend, said I.
Pause and pace, and stop to look by.
A million faces, in spaces around.
There, through free will and wanting, go I.

Feminine spirit, Warrior guise
Open to the magic of life and surprise.
There, through free will and wanting, go I.
Darkness knows no conclusion, but light.

There through free will and wanting, go I.
All as it needs to be know I.

ME, MYSELF AND I

I beared a child on my HIPS
I held mans love in my HEART
Craddled dying Mother in my ARMS
Stroked sick Father with my HANDS

I nursed my BELLY full of dis-ease
I laughed my FACE off
And cried salty tears from my EYES

I bore milk from my BREAST
I walked for miles on weary FEET
I stretched my BACK in asanas
And held my HEAD in despair,
and Up in pride

I fought back with a MOUTHy sting
I consoled with a hearty SMILE
I threw my HAIR back in passion
And fell to my KNEES in hurt

But the longer I live
In this body I call mine
The easier it becomes
To see that I have played
a wonderful game
Called Life

And though my body is my temple
My SOUL is the essence
And everything I've been
And all those memories of WOMAN
I'll leave behind

DIVINE FEMININE

Divine Feminine needs
Divine Masculine
To hold space
For Her
To express herself
Fully and Wildly

Divine Feminine needs
Divine Masculine
To protect her energy
To create space
For his leadership

Him the ship
Her the ocean
She nurtures, loves, connects
He supports and transforms

Divine feminine needs
Divine Masculine
To lay the foundation
For her to reveal herself
To him
To show him Home

Hold her
And she'll hold you
Give her the Sun
And she'll give you the Moon

BROWN SKINNED LADY

He told me to listen to this song
And I heard what he was saying
Through the lyrical genius of another
He resonated and vibrated

Brown Skinned Lady
He returned the gesture
Of the poetry his presence ignited
I'm so fine with it, and I listen

So the Brown Skinned Man I wrote about
Becomes the Brown Skinned Lady he dreams about
Synchronicity of different shades of brown
Heady, heavy, hedonistic and high

Seducing through song and lyrical genius
Through communicating and imagining
Dreaming and meditating on presence
From the surreal to the sublime

We climb the heady heights
Of the unknown landscape of who knows
Fusing ideals, bonding hearts
Ocean and Land keeping us apart

I ail, he rides, we talk, all the time
Time differences unreal
We sync in spaces and heal
He rises, I sleep and every so often not

What's to be of this who knows
We flow, we vibe, ride the wave of union
Don't know how
Don't know when

And then it fades.

THE SOVEREIGN WOMAN

The Rising Woman wades through the deep
To see the Light within
The Rising Woman swims through the mirk
Where the waterlily is King
The rising woman breaks through the carbon
To catch that Diamond win

She cannot rise, except from below
The ground in which she roots
 She cannot rise without despair
At her feet, is where buds shoot

To transform her suffering into sacred
That woman, she will find Grace
To say "I see you pain, and I'm here with you"
She'll flow through time and space

If she can let go of her fettered self
And see through her conditioned state
That woman there will rise indeed
Her presence will be so great

The path of the warrior is the path she takes
That to welcome herself home
to keep coming back to the sanctuary within
That's the sign of a woman who's grown

To bleed and sweat and cry tears of pain
To hold herself throughout
To turn her yearning into devotion
Is the Rising Woman's clout

She gives permission to be as she is
She lays down her sword and fight
As a phoenix rises, wings wide open
The Rising Woman takes flight

A woman rising liberates herself
From the clutches of all those fears
She stands in presence at all she's seen
Her journey made of tears

She's proud of all she has become
And all that she is not
She's knows the common experience
That everyone else forgot

In her eyes you see her Truth
You see her unfettered soul
That Diamond light that shines within
That makes her seem so whole

There is no fear in her experience
She's here to have it all
She asks that you see into her
So that into your Heart you fall

And THAT is intimacy, you know
In To Me You See
Because She is You and You are Her
It's all that you can BE

She quietens her mind so well
So that her heart may speak
She knows it's the most tranquil place
Where life is no longer bleak

This woman chooses not to live in pain
Except to pass through with Grace
She knows she deserves a second chance
To grow this beautiful place

This - the place she calls her Home
The place that no-one knows
The place where only she can go
Where only her garden grows

The Rising Woman is all there is
So sovereign and so True
She rose out of ashes you see
She wove Gold from all the blue

The Rising Woman wades through the deep
To see the Light within
The Rising Woman swims through the mirk
Where the waterlily is King
The rising woman breaks through the carbon
To catch that Diamond win

MAGPIE

I meditated this morning
Sat silent on my bed
Until a knock on my window
Made me look to my left

There perched beside me
Was a magpie of all things
Tapping on my window
Calling at me

The spirit totem of magpie
Calls on thee for courage
Be brave, be creative
Don't hide from the world!

A symbol of duality
Black and white is he
Good Morning Mr Magpie!
What does he say to me?

TOO THIS TOO THAT

I was called the Ugly One
As though the value of my existence
Was measured against someone else
In the eyes of my perpetrators

As though their perception of me
Defined me
Because without their truth
I did not belong in the world

I was called too fat
As though someone else's body size
Was the barometer for my existence

I was called too dark
As though my tone was too offensive
For the fairer more beautiful people

I carried the weight of their stifled pain
Until the dawn of my adulthood
Until I came to realize that their pain
Need not be mine

I came to see that their judgements
Were the reflections of their own mirrors
The ancestral trauma handed down
and blindly accepted

And then I was born!
Little, fat, dark, ugly old me!
Low and behold the truth of nightmares
Born and living before their very eyes

And then I was born! Again!
To break the cycle of the pain
Of the bullshit that sold me down the river
Like a piece of driftwood cast away

And I rose in defiance and realization
That I could release their trauma
And heal generations of women

So I do the work! I delve into the pain
Into the ugly hurt and anger
Into the very pit of my betrayal
Into the very heart of my rejection

I stand before you as Enough
I stand before you as mighty
And as tall as an old oak tree
In spirit!

I am here. I am now. I am fierce.
I am allowed. I have permission.
To exist let alone to stand proud.

I have nothing to prove anymore
My divine presence is enough
I am far from perfect in the eyes of mere beings
My own reflection throwing dissatisfaction
At me every day

But I am nothing but perfect
In the cosmic nature of all things
Here as I am because I am enough
Far greater than family or creed
Pure in the eyes of the Divine

I laugh in the eyes of mere mortals
Who think they have the truthful answers
To the value of my existence
They know not themselves let alone me

I am nothing in the grand scheme of living things
But everything as the fragment of consciousness
I am enough!

Boundless and bigger than the confines of my form
More powerful than the space I hold within
Brighter than my brown
That might fool people
Into thinking I can't radiate light!

BLACK HISTORY

I am Sri Lankan. I am British
I am not White or English
I'm not the exotic thing
That is so unusual to you

A thousand miles to the East
A thousand miles to the West
I could step outside to
prejudice or biased love

Some say I am a coconut
Brown outside and white inside
Not one or the other
A little bit of brown
And a little bit of white

Black men call me sexy
White men call me exotic
Asian men call me a traitor
And I call myself Janaki

I dated black men and married white
Brown men said I was too dark
I couldn't stomach their prejudice
So I got prejudiced too

That I should let the judgement of few
Cast a shadow on the many
Thinking his was the fault of all
The many who shared his skin
His culture, history or pain

I bore a child of mixed heritage
Indigenous Sri Lanka split by war
Dictatorship of Franco's Spain
Depressed, green Emerald Isle
Revolutionist heart of Argentinian land

My child tread the footsteps
Of lands I never dreamed of
Long before she took hold in me
Because I loved the son of immigrants

I can love your porcelain white face
And that fiery thick red hair
Skin riddled in speckles of red dots
And eyes that look like ocean

Just as I can drown in the mystery
Of your black skin shining
In the warm heat
Of a balmy dark night

I have black heroes and sheroes
I have white heroes and sheroes
Friends of all hues
And foes of all shades

I love poets which make me immoral
'If' by imperialist Kipling
Who gave me hope
When my back was on the wall

And Still I Rise by Maya Angelou
Who knew why the caged bird sings
Witness of America's racist South
Who triumphed in civil rights

I am a paler shade of black
Birthed by my ancestors
Just like yours but
You may not like it

Centre of the Earth we hailed
Africa: land of my Mother
Africa: land of my Father
Of many lifetimes ago

I love my brown ass
And so I love you too
No law or time in history
Will turn my heart

I will not let one mans hatred
Allow my heart to sink into hate
I will wait until I can see
The true colour of your character
And then let you in

For I will love that person
Whose heart is made of gold
Whose blood is as red as fire
And who loves without concern

And I will learn from all people
And teach from my belly
And you will judge me
Because I am brown

Because I am not White
I am a shade of black
In my heart and in my skin
Just like You.

BREATHE

She tries so hard
To catch her breath!
So close, so near
Whoosh!

She gasps with panic
That elusive breath!
Squeezing her lungs
Tight in bondage

Breath leaving her breathless
Oh! The irony
Bitter and cruel
Teased to oblivion

Is the breath that evades her
The love she never gave
Herself?
That bastard Love

Forcing her presence
Igniting her fear
The promised land
She once knew

Surrender to the unknown
Still here, standing
Feeling it's lost
But still she's here...

If breathing evades her
What keeps her here?
Perception lost?
Faith gone?

Fuck No, she deserves
Her breath
To feel the bellyful
And the chest empty

To know her breath!
To not just trust
In something unseen
Unfelt and unknown

Breathe they tell her
Fuck you
Watch her try!
Watch her labour!

To love herself
So she can have breath
And breathe and sing
And laugh and dance

Oh that elusive breath!
Where does it go?
How does she survive?
Is this the course of life

Weaving her into a new path
Of more pain
Or more liberation
She stands but trembles

Tired, weak and low
But spirit soars
In hope and need
To preserve her

Breath leaving her breathless
Oh! The irony!
Bitter and cruel
Teased and fucked...

HIS NAME

My best friend
He comes sit with me sometimes
Holds me tight
Tells me he's gonna stay

Tickles my belly
Rubs my head good
Gets inside me and
Fucks me hard

Leaves trails in my heart
Empties me
Then fills me up
Talks to me at night

I know him so well
He knows me too
We go through thick and thin
He's by my side

Solid and honest
He keeps it real
Even on floaty
Let's be dreamy days

He's soft too
Gentle, caressing, light
Always by my side
He holds my hand

'til it sweats
He whispers sweet nothings
And sits at the foot of my bed
Till I sleep

He strokes my brow
And watches my tears
Flow through
Trickle down

He let's me be
Just present
When he goes he says
I'll be right back

He strokes my back
And kisses my chest
Till it aches
Then he smiles

He eats me
Till my hairs stand on end
He pins me down
And feeds me too

"Who is he?" you ask
"He sounds unreal" you say
"Oh he is!" I reply

"His name?
 His name is Pain."

SECRET LOVE

I miss the way you chase my lips with yours
The way you hold my face
And look at me with care
I miss your smile
And the stolen kisses in company

I miss your hand on my hip
And the smell of you, divine
I miss that peek inside your shirt
Like I'd find something new
And the anticipation building
It's raw and it's kind

Passionate and wild
I miss the tease and the eyes
The affection and time
The fun and the thrill
A love not returned
But true

He is the secret of time past
My dear and secret love
Known really only to child

DO YOU THINK?

Do you think...
My lips can sing the sweet song of you
Forever? Do you?

Do you think...
That it matters how long
I behold the vision of you
To enjoy your gem?

Let me explain....

Do you think...
When the scent of sweet frangipane lingers
That the joy of it dies the moment I stop
Seeing?

Do you think...
The feel of salty sea air on my face
Dies when the track turns to stone and heath?

Do you think....
The joy of my child's laugh and mucky face
Ends when the woman walks down the aisle?

Do you think...
The mis-spent youth of my carefree self
Fades when the grown woman
finds integrity and grace?

Do you think...
The loves lost prevail
when love is found once more?
Or no more?

Do you think...
The taste of fruit and it's juice dripping down my face
Evades me when I'm ill and off food?

The heady mix of your truth and being
Your vision and presence
Your joy and light
Is cast in stone

Such that long after reality fades
Or space and time passes
Or the sweet truth of us remains
My beach is full

Imprinted on my heart
Placed in my hand
Carried in my belly
Scorched in my mind
My lips...

My lips DO sing the sweet song of you
Forever.
And
Ever.

MY FAVOURITE PERSON

My favourite person of twenty-nineteen
The sweetest song this summer's seen
Insight Timer - meditators are keen
Soul searchers and lovers who wanna come clean

The YouTube songs flew thick and fast
Virtual seduction - we so surpassed
My dating prowess and game went fast
Threw down the gauntlet for this overseas blast

Video calls through the whatsapp app
Glossed up my lips for the virtual chat
Took sexy photos Sat my phone on my lap
The calls came thick and fast like a hot running tap

Got sexy and hellbent on the brown skinned man
Who turned my heart into fine dust and sand
Thought in the UK or Europe he might land
But I found my life in medical hands

Life turned a corner for both of us it seems
Fall came and went in a flash and a beam
Triggered and fucked I fell apart at the seams
Life got a little too real for the team

Who knows where this interaction might fold
As we dip in and out of this fairy-tale gold
Triggered down deep if I may be so bold
As to suggest that you blow hot and cold

But warm is the colour of my bruised ego
I let it flow and hope that the universe might show
That my feelings run deep and my hope doesn't go
Despite the outcomes and the curveballs we throw

Gangaji tells us to stop and slow down
To call off the search and to prevent the drown
Descent into suffering turned my smile to a frown
Then I hear Black Star sing about the lady so brown

Tiny Desk, Sadhguru and Maté
Things keep us connected in talk and play
Friction and sadness and anxiety might stay
But will we meet one fine day?...

ABANDONED

The feel of abandonment
So visceral and real
The smell of abandonment
Is this a done deal?

I know that feeling well
I can hear before it speaks
I sense the falling away
It's gradual and it's bleak

The feigned concern for me
Borne of shame or guilt
I can't decide which.
All the space that we built

My questions unanswered
His life no longer shared
I give him my time
But his energy I'm spared

My vulnerable on the table
I shared my secrets dear
To have them incarcerated
His silence breeds fear

I asked for communication
The kind which he speaks
I gave him my presence
But his heart space, it leaks

I'm hurtin right now
By his inability to care
To share with me his thoughts
To tell me he dares

To capture and let go
It's a patronising game
To think he can withdraw
And leave me without maim?

His pity and concern
Gives me cause for alarm
Why is he pretending?
Why is he causing this harm?

Speak your truth here
Speak it loud and clear
Or else don't bother with me
My worth is quite dear!

It takes a man of courage
To be able to hold
A woman like me
Small, yet made of gold

I give my open heart
But I need the same back
If he can't be that brave
Then it's trust that he lacks

Indeed **it takes two**
To make a thing work
But the day he reminded me
Is the day that he shirked

I laid out my thoughts
I gave a piece of my heart
But honoured it wasn't
To talk? We didn't even start

So what is this love
That he's so curious for?
The love that he ponders
But can't seem to explore

Infatuation? I know it well
The kind I seem to invoke
I hoped it would stick
In a man who is woke

But alas I am wrong!
It's a game of the weak
The ones who excite
And then can't stand the heat

Love isn't a fools game
It's a journey to be made
It's a promise to oneself
To lay your heart by the blade

To risk his inner child
To brave the winds of hope
To know he might get cut
But still be willing to cope

For something that is pure
As the sun is on skin
If there's an ounce of love in you
Sing it like a hymn!

I won't hurt him
I'll never do that
I wouldn't wish him ill
But I need the same back

His silence is cruel
It's loud and it's clear
That energy he gave
It was so very sheer

But now it's a drip
A leaky tap at best
Of short bursts of hello
And then a long rest

I'm not his go-to
When he trips and then chats
I'm here for it all
When he's high and when he's flat

I don't know what this was
I don't know what this is
But I know what I feel
Right now it's not bliss

It was magic for sure
And it was oh so fun
I felt I had landed
On the lap of a good one

Was I just the catalyst?
To get him back feeling zest?
So that he could just dump me
As soon as he's at best?

That's cold and that's mean
And thats certainly not love
I might be his boo
But what is it he speaks of?

What does it mean?
It's a half-hearted way
To say he wanted me in form
But at distance he'll stay

I was all in.
One hundred percent.
That hell yeah he speaks of
But I feel it's been spent

I'm ready to give
To a man who can stand
In front of me with love
Dripping from his hands

The kind that's worthy
Of house and of home
I have so much to give
To my King on his throne

So the tide turns for me
It's angry as fuck
I'm scared as hell right now
All I need is some luck

For something to change
For something to give
So I can start forging
A new life I can live

With courage and growth
Aspiration and passion
I deserve it all
Without an ounce of ashen

A life full of colour
And love and of hope
With a man in my life
Who's woke and who's dope

Until such time
I'll just nurse my sores
Carry on self-caring
Til the day that I roar.

JOE

He's hurtin and frontin
A broke woman in his life
The angry person's drama
Got him all jacked up on strife

There's a love which doesn't ask
For money or marriage or shit
Just time and fucks... given
The kinda love to lift

Elevates joy, neutralises pain
Divine splendour and bliss
She's not messing, not needin
Just wantin that sweet kiss

He knows she knows he knows
Her love and sex is primed
It's sensual – best done neat
No mixer needed – just time

Fuck her for hours on end
Brown, warm and sweet
It's raw and it's hard
Black, chiselled and deep

He knows he can do her right
Like strong women need
She's killing him so slow
He's fucking her at speed

And she's licking a knife of lust
She's sings her sex so loud
He gets her poetry and vibe
His hard body standing proud

She's challenged by Black love
Tryna figure it all out
Knowin her only Black is Brown
Not good enough no doubt

She reads Spirit Of A Man
To try and educate herself
But in the process hurtin
By men who put her on a shelf

Men who see her gentle strength
Who see her subtle worth
But her ask is too much for them
From boy she needs man to birth

It's healing, power and surrender
Let the feminine cast his ship
Giving him the ocean to ride
Her vulnerability can't dip

Her sex can hold and expel
It can birth, contract and yield
It can open it's yoni arms
To give him a home to shield

His pain and anxt of the world
Is something she can bear
But she knows in return
His energy needs to care

To protect her and hold her
Give her the sanctuary she needs
To grow and blossom and bloom
Then from her body he can feed

So where to now you ask?
He wants no strings attached
A relationship of sorts
With a get-out clause to match

So the proud Black man is strong
He can profess all he needs
That his promises can't go long term
It's hurt! Please stop his bleed

So let her take over for now
And hand yourself over to she
Let her taste your sweet mahogany
And devour her - fast and free...

Let the scent of her linger over you
Let her warm caress take reign
Smell her sex and sweet longing
Let your manhood pleasure her pain

HANDSWORTH BOY

Handsworth boy
Self-made but coy
He's flying high
Says he's shy

I wait for him
To make me kin
The wait is long
Is this wrong?

I could give my world
Tender love of a girl
Solace and peace
Tame his wild beast

Humble beginnings
Two souls singing
I see through the veil
Of the strong male

The boy has a soul
Toughened with gold
Hardened with pain
Tender not vain

Emotionally cold
His love isn't bold
Hidden away
I want him to play

To trust me a bit
To see my joy lit
I'm moody he says
Childish ways

How does he know?
When he won't show?
Love doesn't grow
On the down low

My spirit is light
Simple but bright
I'm a Wembley girl
With kink and curl

A heart with soul
A poet with goals
A lover and Mum
Blackened by Sun

Shy and quiet
Sharp and wired
Roars like a lion
On Mount Zion

Strong and subtle
My love is gentle
My heart is pure
But he ain't sure

BROWN SKINNED MAN

Brown-skinned man
Chocolate, cocoa, cinnamon - sweet
Earthy, turmeric and nutmeg too
Melting pot of spice
Nectar chaser
Honey dripping down my throat

Unctious delicious
Right up my street
Warm, balmy nights - star-studded
Do you drip like dew?
Wipe syrup from your brow?
Is your water like wine?
Are you so divine?

Brown-skinned man
Like the grain in wood
A work of art
The shape of you

Is your heart like golden sand?
Run my fingers through it
Touching you
Leaving marks and trails of wonder
Imprints of lust
Poetry in motion

Brown-skinned man
Amber light
Caramel delight
Burn my fire and make it bright

Brown-skinned man
So divine
I want your brown on mine

Molasses, demerera
So, so fine
Pure like grapes on vine

Heavenly sweet
A manly treat
Brown-skinned man
Divine